FEARLESS FAITH

He staggered not at the promise of God through unbelief; but was strong in faith, giving glory to God.

Romans 4:20

by
Franklin N. Abazie

Fearless Faith
COPYRIGHT 2016 BY Franklin N Abazie
ISBN: 978-1-94513305-3

All right reserved. This book or any portion thereof may not be reproduced or used in any manner whatsoever without the express written permission of the publisher, except for the use of brief quotations in a book review. All Bible quotes are from King James Version and others as noted.

Published by: F N ABAZIE PUBLISHING HOUSE—aka, Empowerment Bookstore

*That I may publish with the voice of thanksgiving
and tell of all thy wondrous works.*
Psalms 26:7

To order additional copies, wholesales or booking call:
the Church office (973-372-7518)
or Empowerment Bookstore Hotline (973-393-8518)

Worship address:
343 Sanford Avenue, Newark, New Jersey 07106
Administrative Head Office address:
33 Schley Street Newark New Jersey 07112
Email: pastorfranknto@yahoo.com
Website www.fnabaziehealingministries.org
Publishing House: www.fnabaziepublishinghouse.org

This book is a production of F N Abazie Publishing House. A publication Arms of Miracle of God Ministries 2016.
First Edition

CONTENTS

THE MANDATE OF THE COMMISSION..................iv
ARMS OF THE COMMISSION..................................v
INTRODUCTION..vi
CHAPTER 1
The Mystery of Faith...1
CHAPTER 2
The Power of Faith..11
CHAPTER 3
The Works of Faith..17
CHAPTER 4
Prayer of Salvation..54
CHAPTER 5
About the Author..63

THE MANDATE OF THE COMMISSION

"The moment is due to impact your world through the revival of the healing & miracle ministry of Jesus Christ of Nazareth.

"I am sending you to restore health unto thee and I will heal thee of thy wounds, said the Lord of Host."

ARMS OF THE COMMISSION

1) F N Abazie Ministries—Miracle of God Ministries (Miracle Chapel Intl)

2) F N Abazie TV Ministries: Global Television Ministry Outreach

3) F N Abazie Radio Ministries: Radio Broadcasting Outreach

4) F N Abazie Publishing House: Book Publication

5) F N Abazie Bible School: also called Word of Healing Bible School (W.O.H.B.S.)

6) F N Abazie Evangelistic Ass: Miracle of God Ministries: Global Crusade

7) Empowerment Bookstore: Book distribution

8) F N Abazie Helping Hands: Meeting the Help of the Needy Worldwide

9) F N Abazie Disaster Recovery Mission: Global Disaster Recovery

10) F N Abazie Prison Ministry: Prison Ministry For All Convicts "Second Chance"

Some of our ministry arms are awaiting the appointed time to commence.

INTRODUCTION

Unless we are FEARLESS in life, we will not make a mark in our generation. We live in a time where FEAR and TERROR have taken everyone captive. It is written: *"Thou shalt not be afraid for the terror by night; nor for the arrow that flieth by day; Nor for the pestilence that walketh in darkness; nor for the destruction that wasteth at noonday."* (Psalms 91:5-6)

Most people are so afraid of a terrorist threat that they can no longer function as normally as they used to. We obviously forget that it took DANIEL'S "FEARLESS FAITH" in GOD to subdue the lions inside the lion's DEN. For Shadrach, Meshach and Abednego to survive the burning fiery furnace, FEARLESS FAITH took over the atmosphere. *"If it be so, our God whom we serve is able to deliver us from the burning fiery furnace, and he will deliver us out of thine hand, O king."* (Daniel 3:17)

My God hath sent his angel, and hath shut the lions' mouths, that they have not hurt me: forasmuch as before him innocency was found in me; and also before thee, O king, have I done no hurt.
Daniel 6:22

Fearless faith is the faith that deals with any prevailing life-threatening circumstances. This faith, in my opinion, has no secondhand value nor alternatives in life. It is the faith that says—IF I PERISH, I PERISH. *"And so will I go in unto the king, which is not according to the law: and if I perish, I perish."* (Esther 4:16)

Remember the three Hebrew boys—Shadrach, Meshach and Abednego? It took "fearless faith" for these three boys to disobey the king.

Shadrach, Meshach, and Abednego, answered and said to the king, O Nebuchadnezzar, we are not careful to answer thee in this matter.
Daniel 3:16

Although we live by FAITH, most of us have not been able to apply FEARLESS FAITH into our lives and circumstances. We have neglected and ignored this great mystery of faith that works like fire.

Perhaps out of anxiety or fear of the unknown, we shy away from applying FEARLESS FAITH into all affairs of our lives.

Now faith is the substance of things hoped for, the evidence of things not seen.
Hebrews 11:1

Although fearless faith works by love and the wisdom of God, it takes the POWER and PRESENCE of the HOLY SPIRIT who is the advocate and a representative of the supreme sovereign Power of God for fearless faith to be victorious.

As a representative, the HOLY SPIRIT takes

over our battle—especially when we genuinely provoke FEARLESS FAITH into action. *"Ye shall not need to fight in this battle: set yourselves, stand ye still, and see the salvation of the Lord with you, O Judah and Jerusalem: fear not, nor be dismayed; tomorrow go out against them: for the Lord will be with you."* (2 Chronicles 20:17) *"The Lord shall fight for you, and ye shall hold your peace."* (Exodus 14:14)

FEARLESS FAITH IS A MYSTERY THAT CANNOT BE UNDERSTAND IN THE ENERGY OF THE FLESH

As thou knowest not what is the way of the spirit, nor how the bones do grow in the womb of her that is with child: even so thou knowest not the works of God who maketh all.
Ecclesiastes 11:5

      We will never be able to become successful and outstanding in life unless we provoke the hidden mystery of fearless faith. For fearless faith to manifest in our lives, we must make up our minds and stand strongly behind our decision. If we must overcome the devil, overcome obstacles and dominate sin and poverty in our lifetime, we must operate by fearless faith.

FEARLESS FAITH IS
THE CONQUERING FORCE OF VICTORY

Fearless mentality is the conquering winning Spirit. The reason all animals fear the lion is because of the fearless nature of the lion. It is written: "And one of the elders saith unto me, Weep not: behol*d, the Lion of the tribe of Judah, the Root of David, hath prevailed to open the book, and to loose the seven seals thereof."* (Revelation 5:5) If we must make an impact in these desperate times we live in, we must approach everything around us with a fearless mentality.

Above all, taking the shield of faith, wherewith ye shall be able to quench all the fiery darts of the wicked.
Ephesians 6:16

Unless otherwise stated, FEARLESS FAITH is our winning ticket against all the wiles and schemes of the devil in this race of life. FEARLESS FAITH WORKS BY LOVE AND BY WISDOM. I heard of some horrible stories where African boys, who were IGNORANT and lacked THE WISDOM OF GOD, decided to travel to EUROPE from the desert area of ALGERIA, MOROCCO and LIBYA. They planned to CROSS OVER the RIVER and into SPAIN and ITALY illegally, neglecting the risk involved. This is a suicide attempt—not FEARLESS FAITH—in my opinion.

Every time the SPIRIT of GOD within us

moves us to engage into any risky life attempt, we must double check it by the wisdom of God. I know of a few boys from my village who died out of ignorance. A few others ended up in jail by acting ignorant with the law.

> *Behold, I send you forth as sheep in the midst of wolves: be ye therefore wise as serpents, and harmless as doves.*
> **Matthew 10:16**

GOD wants us to embrace FEARLESS FAITH with the wisdom of GOD in us. Ignorance is an old device of the devil that still works strongly for Satan. GOD wants us all to embrace relevant INFORMATION that will transform our lives and destinies. I used to say—INFORMATION PLUS REVELATION EQUALS REVOLUTION.

Remember…

"Lest Satan should get an advantage of us: for we are not ignorant of his devices." (2 Corinthians 2:11) One of my most admired mentors used to say: "There is no mountain anywhere, everyone's mountain is his/her ignorance."

FEARLESS FAITH IS OUR VICTORY INSURANCE

As long as we apply the mystery of FEARLESS FAITH appropriately, we will definitely overcome the devil—the wicked one. *"For whatsoever is born of God overcometh the world: and this is the victory that overcometh the world, even our faith."* (1 John 5:14)

As long as we are armed with relevant INFORMATION with the REVELATION of GOD'S WORD, we are assured of victory against all trials, tribulations and prevailing obstacles in life. In this desperate, terroristic era, we must become fearless with the help of God to defeat the adversary—the devil. We must all develop a fearless mentality if we are to confront all prevailing battles in our lives.

WE WALK IN LIFE BY FEARLESS FAITH

For we walk by faith, not by sight.
2 Corinthians 5:7

We can only engage in CREATIVE INNOVATION and take adventure to EXPLORE and EXPERIENCE our planet AND improve OUR LIVES by FEARLESS FAITH. As long as we have developed FEARLESS FAITH inside of our heart, the DEVIL WILL NOT BE ABLE TO MANIPULATE US. GOD helps us by our FAITH, while the devil takes advantage of us by our FEAR. In the Bible, Job lost all his WEALTH out of FEAR, while DAVID RECOVERED all out of FAITH. *"For the thing which I greatly feared is come upon me, and that which I was afraid of is come unto me."* (Job 3:25)

And David recovered all that the Amalekites had carried away: and David rescued his two wives. And there was nothing lacking to them, neither small nor great, neither sons nor daughters, neither spoil, nor any thing that they had taken to them: David recovered all.
1 Samuel 30:18-19

REMEMBER...
"But without faith it is impossible to please him: for he that cometh to God must believe that he is, and that he is a rewarder of them that diligently seek him." (Hebrews 11:6) As long as we desire to please GOD in life, we must walk by Faith.

WE STAND BY FAITH

Not for that we have dominion over your faith, but are helpers of: your joy: for by faith ye stand.
2 Corinthians 1:24

A wise man once said, "the eyes that look are many but the eyes that see are few." Everyone thinks they are standing, but just the few of us are really standing by faith. The housing crisis back in 2008 here in America drove some people to fall into DEPRESSION, while others committed suicide.

It takes fearless faith to withstand and overcome financial crisis, divorce, unemployment, death in families, barrenness and mockery. It takes fearless faith to overcome the current INFALTION IN NIGERIA. It takes FEARLESS FAITH to overcome hardship and economic crisis. *"Wherefore take unto you the whole armour of God that ye may be able to withstand in the evil day, and having done all, to stand. Stand therefore, having your loins girt about with truth, and having on the breastplate of righteousness."* (Ephesians 6:13-14)

> *For we wrestle not against flesh and blood,*
> *but against principalities, against powers,*
> *against the rulers of the darkness of this world,*
> *against spiritual wickedness in high places.*
> **Ephesians 6:12**

> *Sufficient unto the day is the evil thereof.*
> **Matthew 6:34**

VICTORY IN LIFE IS EXCLUSIVELY RESERVED FOR THE FEARLESS

This publication, therefore, is a book I thoroughly RELECTED over, with my own life as an example, to conclude that without FEARLESS FAITH, we will never overcome the prevailing challenges and obstacles of life.

As a BELIEVER with little or no finances left from our parents to start life, our own adult life, for example—our greatest area of prevailing challenges—is our finances As you read this book I encourage and admonish you in the Holy Ghost to develop fearless faith to withstand and overcome all prevailing financial predicaments in your life. Be blessed.

HAPPY READING!

HIS DESTINY WAS THE CROSS….

HIS PURPOSE WAS LOVE….

HIS REASON WAS YOU….

Shadrach, Meshach, and Abednego, answered and said to the king, O Nebuchadnezzar, we are not careful to answer thee in this matter.

If it be so, our God whom we serve is able to deliver us from the burning fiery furnace, and he will deliver us out of thine hand, O king.

Daniel 3:16-17

HIGHLIGHTS ON FAITH

WHAT IS FAITH?

The book of Hebrews gives us a clear definition of faith. *"Now faith is the substance of things hoped for, the evidence of things not seen."* (Hebrews 11:1) FEARLESS FAITH, therefore, means to BELIEVE GOD in the unseen—the supernatural and miraculous. It means that GOD will surely make good on His promise by making things happen (change) in our lifetime. In my understanding, fearless faith is the faith that is not afraid of anything whatsoever.

FEARLESS FAITH is the faith that takes risks and breaks protocols, rules and regulations. This is the FAITH that is contrary to all facts and findings. As far as I am concerned, fearless faith is always contradicting and contends with the pundits. This is the faith that says despite all prevailing challenges in our life, GOD will surely help us to OVERCOME those difficulties, challenges and obstacles in our lifetime. *"And blessed is she that believed: for there shall be a performance of those things which were told her from the Lord."* (Luke 1:45) The centurion said, *"But speak the word only, and my servant shall be healed."* (Matthew 8:8)

HOW DOES FAITH COME?

"So then faith cometh by hearing, and hearing by the word of God." (Romans 10:17) When faith comes,

we must be moved into action. *"By faith Noah, being warned of God of things not seen as yet, moved with fear, prepared an ark to the saving of his house; by the he condemned the world, and became heir of the righteousness which is by faith. By faith Abraham, when he was called to go out into a place which he should after receive for an inheritance, obeyed; and he went out, not knowing whither he went."* (Hebrews 11:7-8) But our FAITH on its own cannot help us. We must build our faith by praying in the Holy Ghost. For without praying in the SPIRIT, we cannot BUILD UP OURSELVES. *"But ye beloved, building up your selves on your most holy faith, praying in the Holy Ghost."* (Jude 1:20)

HOW DOES FAITH WORK?

"Faith works by love."

If DANIEL did not LOVE GOD, he would have been devoured by the lions. *"Now God had brought Daniel into favour and tender love with the prince of the eunuchs."* (Daniel 1:9) *"And no manner of hurt was found upon him, because he believed in his God."* (Daniel 6:23)

If JOSEPH did not LOVE GOD, he would have not only ended up in slavery, but he would have died in prison. *"And the Lord was with Joseph, and he was a prosperous man; and he was in the house of his master the Egyptian."* (Genesis 39:2)

*But the Lord was with Joseph,
and shewed him mercy, and gave him favour
in the sight of the keeper of the prison.*
Genesis 39:21

FAITH WORKS BY LOVE

But faith which worketh by love.
Galatians 5:6

Without genuine LOVE of GOD, FEARLESS FAITH will be mere stupidity. It will appear like it's a demonic manipulation when we take some very risky steps in life. *"Foolish Galatians, who hath bewitched you, that ye should not obey the truth, before whose eyes Jesus Christ hath been evidently set forth, crucified among you?"* (Galatians 3:1)

We must therefore develop natural affection for GOD and HIS KINGDOM if we must do great things in our lifetime. *"But seek ye first the kingdom of God, and his righteousness; and all these things shall be added unto you."* (Matthew 6:33)

PRAYER POINTS TO ACTIVATE FEARLESS FAITH

—Father lord, empower my fearless faith, in the name of Jesus.

—Power of God, mightily magnify fearless faith inside of me, in the name of Jesus.

—Blood of Jesus, break me through, in the name of Jesus.

—Heavenly Father, change my story by fearless faith, in the name of Jesus.

—Power of God, reverse my story for good, in the name of Jesus.

—Hand of God, destroy all my persecutors, in the name of Jesus.

—Fire of God, roast all hindering spirit prevailing over my glorious destiny.

—I established jurisdiction over all my given real estate territories, in the name of Jesus.

—Every power causing me to retain frustration and despression. loosen your hold, in the name of Jesus.

—Father God, break the stronghold of sin over my life, in the name of Jesus.

—I proclaim the power of fearless faith to come upon me, in the name of Jesus.

—I receive the mystery of fearless faith, in the name of Jesus.

—I reclaim my destiny by the authority, in the name of Jesus

—I demolish all strongholds holding me hostage from manifesting the glory of the Lord.

—Henceforth I move into my miraclous by the mystery and power of fearless faith, in the name of Jesus.

—I reclaim my stolen heritage, in the mighty name of Jesus.

—I abolish all spells and curses against my life, in the mighty name of Jesus.

—I come against all hindering forces harassing my life and my destiny, in the mighty name of Jesus.

—I proclaim vicory over witches and wizards, in the mighty name of Jesus.

—Holy Ghost, fire revive your works in my life, in the mighty name of Jesus.

—Power of God, change my destiny, in the mighty name of Jesus.

—I burry every demonic coffins harassing my future, in the mighty name of Jesus.

—I destroy all tortoise spirit holding me stagnant, in the mighty name of Jesus.

—Spirit of the living God fall upon me.

—Power of the living God, call upon fire of the living God and crush all my enemies, in the mighty name of Jesus.

—Hand of God, deliver me from the token of liars and diviners.

—I receive the power of fearless faith.

—I move forward by the auothrity of fearless faith. Henceforth I must walk into my supernatural miracles, in the mighty name of Jesus.

CHAPTER 1
THE MYSTERY OF FAITH

Holding the mystery of the faith in a pure conscience.
1 Timothy 3:9

Although the mystery of FEARLESS FAITH is inexplicable in the physical realms, it takes a pure conscience to provoke this great mystery. *"For the Lord seeth not as man seeth; for man looketh on the outward appearance, but the Lord looketh on the heart."* (1 Samuel 16:7) Without a good conscience, we cannot provoke the mystery of fearless faith. As long as you are living in wickedness, this great mystery will not work for you. *"Oh let the wickedness of the wicked come to an end; but establish the just: for the righteous God trieth the hearts and reins."* (Psalms 7:9) You cannot be walking in sin and wickedness, yet expecting the mystery of fearless faith to work for you.

FEARLESS FAITH is a mystery that operates in the only inside, unseen kingdom. The mystery of fearless faith cannot be understood in the ENERGY of the FLESH. The mystery of FEARLESS FAITH, in my opinion, BREAKS BARRIERS. It is a pathfinder mystery with a trailblazing force, breaking through unseen barriers and demolishing strongholds that intend to hinder our lives and destinies.

Chapter 1   The Mystery of Faith

Holding faith, and a good conscience;
which some having put away concerning
faith have made shipwreck.
1 Timothy 1:18

Despite all the preaching and hearing of the word of faith, so many of us have, out of ignorance, misinterpreted and misrepresented the mystery of faith. In my opinion, we cannot be living in sin and wickedness—yet expect the mystery of FEARLESS FAITH to shield us in times of trouble. *"For he that soweth to his flesh shall of the flesh reap corruption; but he that soweth to the Spirit shall of the Spirit reap life everlasting. And let us not be weary in well doing: for in due season we shall reap, if we faint not. As we have therefore opportunity, let us do good unto all men, especially unto them who are of the household of faith."* (Galatians 6:8-10)

And the times of this ignorance God winked at;
but now commandeth all men everywhere to repent.
Acts 17:30

God will not hold you accountable when you did not know the RIGHT THING to do. Although the mystery of faith works only with a pure conscience, GOD can allow some degree of the manifestation of this mystery in times of ignorance (when we did not know better).

And this will we do, if God permit.
For it is impossible for those who were
once enlightened, and have tasted of
the heavenly gift, and were made partakers of
the Holy Ghost, And have tasted the good word of God,
and the powers of the world to come, If they shall fall
away, to renew them again unto repentance; seeing
they crucify to themselves the Son of God afresh,
and put him to an open shame.
Hebrews 6:3-6

HOW DOES FEARLESS FAITH WORK?

THE WORDS OF OUR MOUTH

For verily I say unto you, That whosoever shall say unto this mountain, Be thou removed, and be thou cast into the sea; and shall not doubt in his heart, but shall believe that those things which he saith shall come to pass; he shall have whatsoever he saith.
Mark 11:23

In my opinion, every arrogant word from our mouth is a FEARLESS word of FAITH. Fearless faith requires a great degree of AUDACITY, BOLDNESS, POWER and AUTHORITY. We will not be able to DOMINATE THE ENEMY unless we SPEAK OUT BOLDLY IN FAITH. We should always speak out in FAITH if we desire to see ANYTHING GOOD come to pass in our lifetime. *"Shadrach, Meshach, and Abed-*

nego, answered and said to the king, O Nebuchadnezzar, we are not careful to answer thee in this matter. If it be so, our God whom we serve is able to deliver us from the burning fiery furnace, and he will deliver us out of thine hand, O king." (Daniel 3:16-17)

Briefly, here are a few components of FEARLESS FAITH:

BY BOLDNESS

In order to operate under the anointing of fearless faith, we must be bold in confronting our fears and our enemies. Boldness is a virtue that must be implemented if we are to overcome the challenges and obstacles of life. You cannot operate under the mystery of fearless faith without the spirit of boldness. *"Long time therefore abode they speaking boldly in the Lord, which gave testimony unto the word of his grace, and granted signs and wonders to be done by their hands."* (Acts 14:3)

BY AUTHORITY

As Christians we must walk in authority if we are to triumph against the obstacles of life. Until Jesus gave authority to His disciples ,they could not speak in public. A man/woman of AUTHORITY is a men/women of DIGNITY and POWER. A man of AUTHORITY commands the respect of others.

BY DOMINION

We must dominate and rule in our present environment. *"And God blessed them, and God said unto them, Be fruitful, and multiply, and replenish the earth, and subdue it: and have dominion over the fish of the sea, and over the fowl of the air, and over every living thing that moveth upon the earth."* (Genesis 1:28) We must cultivate a dominion mentality if we are to provoke fearless faith into action.

WHAT IS FEARLESS FAITH?

In my opinion, FEARLESS FAITH is the RISKY FAITH. This is the desperate faith that convinces us to take a risk—at the detriment of our whole life existence. Furthermore, fearless faith is the spirit that grants us the courage and boldness to confront prevailing challenges. FEARLESS FAITH is the FAITH that challenges and stretches us beyond our human limitations. It is the *"if I perish, I perish FAITH."* (Esther 4:16)

FEARLESS FAITH is the FAITH that says "I dare you." This is the faith that takes healthy risks, to the detriment of life. FEARLESS FAITH literally brings GOD DOWN to PROTECT and DELIVER us from trouble, from evil forces, from hardship situations, from tribulations and terror. This FAITH moves the SPIRIT OF GOD. This faith moves mountains. "For God hath not given us the spirit of fear; but of power, and of love, and of a sound mind." (2 Timothy 1:7) *"Even those who by reason of use have their senses exercised to discern both good and evil."* (Hebrews 5:14)

Although some ignorant people apply this FAITH foolishly, we are admonished by the HOLY

BIBLE to use our discernment. We are encouraged to exercise wisdom when operating under THE SPIRIT OF FEARLESS FAITH.

Although they may not all be BELIEVERS OR RELIGIOUS PEOPLE, most successful men and women today around the world applied the mystery of FEARLESS FAITH to DOMINATE their world. FEARLESS FAITH, therefore, can be applied everywhere in the world.

In my understanding, FEARLESS FAITH is our ability to be determined to make it in life. FEARLESS FAITH operates by a self-will, power, determination from the heart, strength, endurance, ability to absorb tragedy, hardship, trials, obstacles and other unknown challenges in life. FEARLESS FAITH has zero tolerance for fear.

It is either FAITH OR FEAR. Although we do almost everything in life by faith, we fail to apply faith in everything we engage ourselves in. *"And he that doubteth is damned if he eat, because he eateth not of faith: for whatsoever is not of faith is sin."* (Romans 14:23)

With FEARLESS FAITH we can get results anywhere it is applied in the world. Jesus said to those two blind men in the book of Matthew: *"Then touched he their eyes, saying, According to your faith be it unto you."* (Matthew 9:29) *"And he said unto him, Arise, go thy way: thy faith hath made thee whole."* (Luke 17:19)

FEARLESS FAITH has divine potent power—MEANING THE ABILITY TO WITHSTAND ANY COUNTEROFFENSIVE FORCES. This force has the ability to protect and to deliver, to build and to plant, to throw down and to manifest known objects and unknown inanimate objects in the Earthly realm. DANIEL became a celebrity and witnessed four sitting presidents come and go because of FEARLESS FAITH. FEARLESS FAITH brought the three Hebrew boys into prominence. *"Then the king promoted Shadrach, Meshach, and Abednego, in the province of Babylon."* (Daniel 3:30)

Everyone who speaks boldly is a man or woman of AUTHORITY. Naturally, everyone who has developed FEARLESS FAITH speaks with boldness—and BOLDNESS is the gateway into SIGNS and WONDERS. *"Long time therefore abode they speaking boldly in the Lord, which gave testimony unto the word of his grace, and granted signs and wonders to be done by their hands."* (Acts 14:3)

WHAT ARE THE HINDRANCES TO FAITH?

Here are my 7 definition of fears.

What is fear?

F.....FALSE
E........EXPERIENCE
A..........APPEARING
R.............REAL

F......FACELESS
E........ENEMY
A..............AFFLICTING
R...................REASONING

F.......FREQUENTLY
E..........EXPECTED
A..............ADVERSITY
R..................REALIZED

F........FANTASIZED
E..........EXAGGERATION
A...............ABOVE
R.....................REALITY

F......FIERCE
E.........EMOTION
A.............AROUSING
R..................RESTLESSNESS.

F.......FACELESS
E...........EXPRESSION
A..............ACKNOWLEDGED
R......................REPEATEDLY

F.......FAILURE
E...........EXPECTED
A...............AND
R.......................REHEARSED

Unless we confront our fears, there is no way we can activate the spirit of fearless faith. *"There were they in great fear, where no fear was: for God hath scattered the bones of him that encampeth against thee: thou hast put them to shame, because God hath despised them."* (Psalms 53:5)

ANOTHER HINDRANCE OF FEARLESS FAITH

INTIMIDATION

As long as we are intimidated, we cannot go far in life. We are admonished by the scripture to never allow anybody or any circumstance to intimidate our lives. It is written: *"Weeping may endure for a night, but joy cometh in the morning."* (Psalms 30:5) Remember Jesus said: *"These things I have spoken unto you, that in me ye might have peace. In the world ye shall have tribulation: but be of good cheer; I have overcome the world."* (John 16:33)

Remember, fearless faith is an ever-forward mentality.

"There is a way up for you."

"There is a way forward for you."

"There is a way out for you."

SUMMARY OF CHAPTER ONE

—Fearless faith is the dominating faith.

—Fearless faith is not scared or intimidated by circumstance or persons.

—Fearless faith is the winning faith.

—Fearless faith is the possibility mentality.

CHAPTER 2
THE POWER OF FAITH

Who are kept by the power of God through faith unto salvation ready to be revealed in the last time.
1 Peter 1:5

WHAT ARE WE SAYING?

Faith in God is all we need in life to survive all the wiles and schemes of the devil. *"And Jesus answering saith unto them, Have faith in God."* (Mark 11:22) Every spoken word of faith carries the supernatural backing of the Most High God. *"I form the light, and create darkness: I make peace, and create evil: I the Lord do all these things."* (Isaiah 45:7) Whenever faith is properly appropriated and activated, it has a remarkable effect on our lives. Fearless faith transforms an individual's life from maudlin, common everyday activities to a symphony of joy and happiness.

Our ability to exercise fearless faith in our lives is significant to fulfilling God's plan and original purpose for us. But faith unto salvation is centered on the Lord Jesus Christ, faith in His doctrines and teachings. Unless something strange happens, we will never discover hidden characteristics and traits that transform our lifestyle. Our ability to adapt and endure hardship and prevailing difficult challenges brings out the spirit of fearless faith in us all. *"And his name through faith in his name hath made this man strong, whom ye see and know: yea, the faith which is by him hath given him this perfect soundness in the presence of you all."* (Acts 3:16)

Faith is the arsenal that we must explore in life without any reservations if we are to succeed in life. Fearless faith means to go fully all out, with full conviction, despite all odds. To "have faith" means to be fully-confident, fully-persuaded or fully-convinced that something good is going to occur.

FEARLESS FAITH REQUIRES ACTION

Faith is taking the first step even when you don't see the whole staircase."
Martin Luther King Jr.

Whatever we call faith is not faith unless we apply a corresponding action into our lives. Most of the time we lack corresponding actions to take a giant step in our lives. We will never attain our next level in life without appropriate actions of faith. This action is fearless faith in display. Fearless faith is the moving faith—the moving faith is the now faith. And the now faith is the action faith. *"Yea, a man may say, Thou hast faith, and I have works: shew me thy faith without thy works, and I will shew thee my faith by my works."* (James 2:18)

FEARLESS FAITH BREAKS PROTOCOLS AND DELIVERS THE IMPOSSIBLE

Unless there is a catastrophic challenge, we will never explore the hidden traits inside of our hearts. As a believer, there are a lot of things we have been exempted from by reason of the blood of Jesus. But if something is to happen to our lives, we must rise up with fearless faith to confront it.

Peter was approaching Jesus with fearless faith, walking on the water until he switched into the natural realm, when he became afraid of the sea. *"And Peter answered him and said, Lord, if it be thou, bid me come unto thee on the water. And he said, Come. And when Peter was come down out of the ship, he walked on the water, to go to Jesus. But when he saw the wind boisterous, he was afraid; and beginning to sink, he cried, saying, Lord, save me."* (Matthew 14:28-30)

> *Without faith a man can do nothing;*
> *with it all things are possible.*
> **Sir William Osler**

WHAT DO WE MEAN?

The faith we are talking about is our ability to withstand great pressure and criticism from opposition, our ability to survive unemployment, rejection, loneliness, depression, anger, envy, stress-related jobs, divorce, mental sickness, etc. Fearless faith encourages us to confront and destroy any appearance of fear—either in our dreams or in real-life experience. As a man/woman of fearless faith, every evil dream from the coven of witches must not harass us. Fearless faith releases the dominating spirit that confronts and conquers all such nightmares.

> *You block your dream when you allow your fear*
> *to grow bigger than your faith.*
> **Mary Manin Morrissey**

Without being fully convinced that what you want to happen is about to happen, you won't take the steps necessary to make it happen. When you believe something is going to happen, you get prepared, you start making little changes in anticipation of what is about to happen. This anticipation helps make us modify and adapt as we get ready for the pending new thing into our lives. Fearless faith engages us to be very strong and courageous concerning the outcome of our futures.

Although Satan uses fear to attack our lives, God also uses faith to encourage us against the wiles and schemes of the devil. Faith and fear work opposite to each other. *"For the thing which I greatly feared is come upon me, and that which I was afraid of is come unto me. I was not in safety, neither had I rest, neither was I quiet; yet trouble came."* (Job 3:25-26)

> *Faith is a bird that feels dawn breaking*
> *and sings while it is still dark.*
> **Rabindranath Tagore**

*Understand to achieve anything requires
faith and belief in yourself, vision, hard work,
'determination and dedication. Remember all things
are possible for those who believe.*
Gail Devers

THE BENEFITS OF FEARLES FAITH

—Fearless faith is a gateway into our long-awaited breakthrough in life.

—Fearless faith delivers us from the roaring of the devil.

—Fearless faith guarantees outstanding success in life.

—Fearless faith breaks yokes and limitations.

—Fearless faith is never afraid of anyone or any group of people.

Develop fearless faith today. I once heard President Obama say that he knows what he is doing and he is "fearless." It was fearless faith that helped make Barack Obama the first black president of the United States. Embrace the Spirit of fearless faith and impact your world. Unless you become fearless in all things in life, you will not go far. If you failed before, it does not mean you are a failure.

I define F A I L as—

F ......FIRST
A.........ATTEMPT
I...............IN
L..................LEARNING.

> *I would rather err on the side of faith
> than on the side of doubt.*
> **Robert Schuller**

CHAPTER 3
THE WORK OF FAITH

Jesus answered and said unto them, This is the work of God, that ye believe on him whom he hath sent.
John 6:29

Now thanks be unto God, which always causeth us to triumph in Christ, and maketh manifest the savour of his knowledge by us in every place.
2 Corinthians 2:14

In my understanding, faith is always associated with victory in life. The same way the devil works with your fear, that is how God works with our Faith. Every work of faith must be accompanied by the manifestation of victory. It is written: *"But thanks be to God, which giveth us the victory through our Lord Jesus Christ."* (1 Corinthians 15:57) Whatever we call faith is not faith unless there is victory attached to it. Fearless faith has zero tolerance for defeat, rejection, failure, hatred, malice, envy, depression, stress, etc.

Yea, a man may say, Thou hast faith, and I have works: shew me thy faith without thy works, and I will shew thee my faith by my works.
James 2:18

WHAT IS THE WORK OF FAITH?

FOR FAITH TO WORK, WE MUST BELIEVE IN THE LORD JESUS CHRIST

It is written: *"What shall we do that we might work the works of God? This is the work of God that you believe on him whom he has sent."* (John 6:28-29) Recall with me also, *"These things have I written unto you that believe on the name of the Son of God; that ye may know that ye have eternal life, and that ye may believe on the name of the Son of God."* (1 John 5:13) As long as we put our trust in God, the work of faith is obligated to follow us in life. Remember—*"whatsoever is not of faith is sin."* (Romans 14:23) We must also live a life that reflects on our Christian faith. We must live a life of faith by the help of the Holy Spirit. It is written: *"The life which I now live in the flesh I live by the faith of the Son of God, who loved me, and gave himself for me."* (Galatians 2:20)

HOW DO WE WORK ON OUR FAITH

But ye, beloved, building up yourselves on your most holy faith, praying in the Holy Ghost, Jude1:20. Prayer thanksgiving, and supplication is our only known channel to provoke the works of faith. We must call upon his Holy name in time of trouble and in times of peace. It is written for by faith we stand.
2 Corinthians 1:24

WE MUST FIGHT THE FIGHT OF FAITH

It is written: *"Fight the good fight of faith, lay hold on eternal life, whereunto thou art also called, and hast professed a good profession before many witnesses."* (1 Timothy 6:12)

Fearless faith demands that we put up a fight against the adversary. We must confront every prevailing challenge opposing and hindering our lives. In my opinion, our daily life experience is more or less an experience of conflict. Without the spirit of fearless faith, we will be defeated and subdued by the wicked one—the devil.

We must fight against besetting sins; against the snares and temptations laid every moment for our feet; against the daily unceasing influence of an ungodly world; against the very things that our carnal heart most fondly loves; and against the workings and arguments of our natural mind, which are all opposed to a life of faith. It is written: *"For we wrestle not against flesh and blood, but against principalities, against powers, against the rulers of the darkness of this world, against spiritual wickedness in high places."* (Ephesians 6:12)

LIFE IS A WARFARE AND NOT A FUN FARE

Unless you are ready to fight, you will forever remain defeated in life. Life is full of attacks and assaults from the camp of the devil. Unless we develop a spirit of fearless faith to confront anyone and anything that comes our way in life, we will never be victorious Christians. As a man/woman of faith, I challenge you to wake up and confront all your fears in life. You will not go too far in life without the spirit of fearless faith. You will not make much impact in your lifetime unless you develop a life of fearless faith. Therefore, rise up and confront all the prevailing challenges opposing and hindering your life, in the mighty name of Jesus Christ. Amen.

HEALING KEYS

1) Always carry a positive mindset, regardless of the prevailing circumstances.

2) Always tell yourself the truth before you lie about it.

3) If the truth be told, you are a branch of His blessings, the planting of the Lord.

4) Never confess that you are sick to the hearing of the member of your body.

5) Positive confession with faith yields positive results.

6) Every cures of man have no power to prevail over your life.

7) A merry heart is medicinal and health to your body.

8) Spiritual and emotional well-being is vital to happiness in life.

9) To avoid depression, never have regrets.

10) Never be anxious in life to avoid anxiety.

11) Always live today for today to be at peace with your spirit and with God.

12) You're unique because your challenges are tailored

to you only.

13) The blessing always dominates the curses any day.

14) Decisions are the wheels of life.

15) We either ride into fame or into shame.

16) Daily exercise and some reading of the Bible gurantees good health.

17) Every day is God's day. No day created by God is a disapointment.

18) Stay away from sweet stuff—they are temporary.

19) Sugar is sweet to your taste, beware! It also contributes to diabetes.

20) A good prayer life gurantees longivity.

21) People that pray in tongues do not develop mental disease.

22) Always be positive in everything.

23) Always have a mentor in life that will oppose and fight the tormentor.

24) Always have someone in life to learn from.

25) Tell everybody what you plan to do and someone will help you do it.

26) Winners fight to the last.

27) Quitters never win in life.

28) Soul winners are heirs to the kingdom of god.

29) Soul winners never lack help.

30) Soul winners are cerified with divine help.

31) God is always looking for soul winners to bless.

32) Life is a warfare and not a funfare.

33) In life you fight for all you possess.

34) No man or woman was born rich.

35) In your lifetime do something positive to impact your world.

36) Take care of your life today—you don't have one to spare.

37) Take your life serious before the devil take you down.

38) Always be cheerful at all times.

39) Regardless of the prevailing circumstances around you, your life is in the hand of God.

40) God is the super surgeon that will spiritually-surgically heal you.

41) Always expect help from above and not from abroad.

42) Man will disappoint you, but god will appoint you.

43) The joy of the lord is always our strength.

44) Spiritual height is not measured in length or breath.

45) If you go deeper with God, you will see deeper.

46) Your next level in life is full of recognition.

47) Go to where you are celebrated and not where you are tolerated.

48) Develop yourself in the area of your calling in life.

49) A lifestyle of thanks given keeps God 24/7 on duty on our behalf.

50) Develop a lifestyle of thanksgiving.

51) Thanksgiving guarantees our access to obtain the promises.

WHAT IS INWARD SIN?

"For from within, out of the heart of men, proceed evil thoughts, adulteries, fornications, murders, Thefts, covetousness, wickedness, deceit, lasciviousness, an evil eye, blasphemy, pride, foolishness: All these evil things come from within, and defile the man." (Mark 7:21-23) *"Now we know that God heareth not sinners: but if any man be a worshipper of God, and doeth his will, him he heareth."* (John 9:31)

Every sin that we really never committed but we thought about in our heart—if we engaged our heart on it—it is called inward sin. Oftentimes, if not death, this sin easily besets us.

WHAT IS OUTWARD SIN?

Galatians paints a graphic picture for us. It is written: *"Now the works of the flesh are manifest, which are these; Adultery, fornication, uncleanness, lasciviousness, Idolatry, witchcraft, hatred, variance, emulations, wrath, strife, seditions, heresies, Envyings, murders, drunkenness, revellings, and such like: of the which I tell you before, as I have also told you in time past, that they which do such things shall not inherit the kingdom of God."* (Galatians 5:20)

WHO IS A SINNER?

Know ye not, that to whom ye yield yourselves servants to obey, his servants ye are to whom ye obey; whether of sin unto death, or of obedience unto righteousness.
Romans 6:16

We are all sinners. Every immoral thing you get excited about doing is what makes you a sinner.

Examine yourselves, whether ye be in the faith; prove your own selves. Know ye not your own selves, how that Jesus Christ is in you, except ye be reprobates?
2 Corinthians 13:5

Although most faith people live in denial about the work of the flesh, from my own scriptural understanding, everyone operating within the scope of Galatians 5:20-21 is classified as a sinner.

Now the works of the flesh are manifest, which are these; Adultery, fornication, uncleanness, lasciviousness, idolatry, witchcraft, hatred, variance, emulations, wrath, strife, seditions, heresies, envyings, murders, drunkenness, revellings, and such like: of the which I tell you before, as I have also told you in time past, that they which do such things shall not inherit the kingdom of God.
Galatians 5:20-21

Further supporting scripture...

*But the fearful, and unbelieving,
and the abominable, and murderers,
and whoremongers, and sorcerers, and idolaters,
and all liars, shall have their part in the lake
which burneth with fire and brimstone:
which is the second death.*
Revelation 21:8

UNBELIEVERS

In my view, all that have not acknowledged Jesus Christ as Lord and savior are sinners. It is written: *"But he that believeth not shall be damned."* (Mark 16:16) Remember, *"heareth not sinners."* (John 9:31) In my scriptural understanding, all unbelievers are sinners.

LIARS

All liars are sinners before the Almighty God. Lying is a very serious sin simply because it leads to poverty and shame. Lying decays great destiny and erodes potential future. Someone whom I know very well lies so much to themselves, they became a beggar by paralyzing their future and frustrating the will of God over their life.

HOW DO I COME OUT OF SIN?

The Apostle Paul said in Romans: *"But I see another law in my members, warring against the law of my mind, and bringing me into captivity to the law of sin which is in my members. O wretched man that I am! who shall deliver me from the body of this death? I thank God through Jesus Christ our Lord. So then with the mind I myself serve the law of God; but with the flesh the law of sin."* (Romans 7:23-25) We must therefore be provoked by faith to come out of sin. We must make up our mind that sin shall not have dominion over us again henceforth. Regardless of how you see it, it takes a strong will and decision to come out of a sinful lifestyle. We must therefore make up our minds and stop sin immediately before it erodes our destiny.

You must **REPENT**, **CONFESS** and **PROCLAIM** the LORD JESUS CHRIST. The word says as many as received him, to them gave He power to become the sons of God. Even to them that believe on his name.

To qualify for divine visitation, do the following (with sincerity):

1) ***Acknowledge*** that you are a sinner and that He died for you. (Romans 3:23)

2) ***Repent of your sins***. (Acts 3:19, Luke 13:5, 2 Peter 3:9)

3) ***Believe in your heart*** that Jesus died for your sin. (Romans 10:10)

4) ***Confess Jesus as the Lord over your life.*** (Romans 10:10, Acts 2:21)

Now repeat this Prayer after me—

Say Lord Jesus, I accept you today, as my Lord and my savior, forgive me of my sins wash me with your blood. Right now, I believe, I am sanctified, I am save, I am free, I am free from the Power of sin to serve the Lord Jesus. Thank you Lord for saving me. Amen.

Congratulations.

YOU ARE NOW A BORN AGAIN CHRISTIAN!

STEPS TO OVERCOME THE LIFESTYLE OF SIN

FAITH

FAITH is the living FORCE that will DELIVER US all from SIN. We must therefore BELIEVE in the FINISHED WORK OF JESUS CHRIST on the CROSS. Whenever FAITH steps into any life, there is always proof of transformation. *"And be not conformed to this world: but be ye transformed by the renewing of your mind, that ye may prove what is that good, and acceptable, and perfect, will of God."* (Romans 12:2) Therefore, develop faith that will destroy all SINFUL HABITS IN YOUR LIFE.

PRAYER

We are admonished in the scripture that the only way to build up our FAITH IS BY PRAYING IN THE SPIIRT. Most of the relief and assurance that will come into our lives is on the platform of prayers. The significance of prayer cannot be over emphasized. PRAYER IS SO POWERFUL THAT IT WILL GIVE YOU HOPE. Most of us complain about challenges, but never create the time to pray about it. We tell everybody about it—but we do not tell God about it. Every time we really talk to GOD in PRAYERS, the devil knows.

DECISION KEYS

1) Nothing changes until you make up your mind.

2) Decision is the gateway to deliverance.

3) Until you decide, no one will decide for you.

4) Your prosperity is proportional to your decisions.

5) The decision you make will determine the future you will create

6) Decision creates future and fulfills destinies.

7) Decision beautifies our future.

8) Decision keeps you out of trouble.

9) Decision exempts you from evil.

10) Decision gurantees eternity.

11) You can only go far in life by your faith decisions.

12) You are poor because you made such decisions

13) Make a decision and change your life.

14) Life changing decisions are a function of quality information.

15) Success in life is a function of decision.

16) Life experiences are full of decisions.

17) Decisions change destinies.

18) Never settle for information—always look for revelation.

19) You are where you are today based on your last decision.

20) Information is crucial in decision making.

21) Decision makers rule the world.

22) You can rule your world with quality decisions.

23) As long as you decide rightly, Satan cannot harrass you.

CONDITIONS TO RECEIVE THE HOLY SPIRIT

If we are to receive the help of the precious Holy Spirit, we must do the following:

REPENTANCE
We must repent of all our sins and our wicked ways in life. Repentance is the initial step into healing and restoration. *"Repent, and be baptized every one of you in the name of Jesus Christ for the remission of sins, and ye shall receive the gift of the Holy Ghost."* (Acts 2:38)

BE BAPTIZED
As a child of God, we must be baptized. *"Be baptized every one of you in the name of Jesus Christ for the remission of sins, and ye shall receive the gift of the Holy Ghost."* (Acts 2:38)

CONFESS OF YOUR SIN
Although we must confess our sins, we must also confess that Jesus is Lord—otherwise we remain subject to the devil territory. *"If we confess our sins, He is faithful and just to forgive us our sins, and to cleanse us from all unrighteousness."* (1 John 1:9)

ACKNOWLEDGEMENT
Acknowledge that you are a sinner and that Jesus Christ died for your sins. (Romans 3:23)

BORN AGAIN
We must be born again.

CONFRONTING PREVAILING CHALLENGES IN THE MIDST OF GREAT HARDSHIP AND DIFFICULTIES

These things I have spoken unto you, that in me ye might have peace. In the world ye shall have tribulation: but be of good cheer; I have overcome the world.
John 16:33

In our lifetime we will face strong opposition, contenders and confrontation as long as we live and exist. No matter how careful you may try to avoid confronting your fears and troubles, it will confront you if you do not confront it and face it first. It is written:

There hath no temptation taken you but such as is common to man: but God is faithful, who will not suffer you to be tempted above that ye are able; but will with the temptation also make a way to escape, that ye may be able to bear it.
1 Corinthians 10:13

Great Biblical characters like Gideon, Samson, David and Caleb were men who endured great difficulties and faced harsh opposition—yet confronted and conquered all their enemies in their lifetimes.

Have not I commanded thee? Be strong and of a good courage; be not afraid, neither be thou dismayed: for the Lord thy God is with thee whithersoever thou goest.
Joshua 1:9

And Caleb stilled the people before Moses, and said, Let us go up at once, and possess it; for we are well able to overcome it. But the men that went up with him said, We be not able to go up against the people; for they are stronger than we. And they brought up an evil report of the land which they had searched unto the children of Israel, saying, The land, through which we have gone to search it, is a land that eateth up the inhabitants thereof; and all the people that we saw in it are men of a great stature. And there we saw the giants, the sons of Anak, which come of the giants: and we were in our own sight as grasshoppers, and so we were in their sight.
Numbers 13:30-33

The above biblical quotation should inspire everyone. Remember...

"What you do not want, you don't watch."

"What you do not resist has power to remain."

"What you do not confront, you cannot conquer."

We must therefore be willing to confront all our fears and worries in life. It is written: *"But thanks be to God, which giveth us the victory through our Lord Jesus Christ. Therefore, my beloved brethren, be ye stedfast, unmoveable, always abounding in the work of the Lord, forasmuch as ye know that your labour is not in vain in the Lord."* (1 Corinthians 15:57-58)

Let's briefly examine the prerequisites to overcoming trials and tribulations in life.

BE BORN AGAIN

We must be willing to confront every opposition in life. As simple as SALVATION may appear, we must recognize that there is a Spirit and a force that changes our status as children of the Living God.

Jesus answered and said unto him, Verily, verily, I say unto thee, Except a man be born again, he cannot see the kingdom of God. Nicodemus saith unto him, How can a man be born when he is old? can he enter the second time into his mother's womb, and be born? Jesus answered, Verily, verily, I say unto thee, Except a man be born of water and of the Spirit, he cannot enter into the kingdom of God. That which is born of the flesh is flesh; and that which is born of the Spirit is spirit. Marvel not that I said unto thee, Ye must be born again. The wind bloweth where it listeth, and thou hearest the sound thereof, but canst not tell whence it cometh, and whither it goeth: so is every one that is born of the Spirit.
John 3:3-8

WE MUST PRACTICE RIGHTEOUSNESS AS A LIFE STYLE

It is written: *"And who is he that will harm you, if ye be followers of that which is good?"* (1 Peter 3:13)

Remember…

"Whoso keepeth the commandment shall feel no evil thing: and a wise man's heart discerneth both time and judgment." (Ecclesiastes 8:5)

We must embrace righteousness as a lifestyle if we are to make an impact in our lifetime. We must stand up for what we believe, confront our fears and live a righteous life.

PRAYER POINTS TO OVERCOME TRIALS BY THE HELP OF THE HOLY SPIRIT

1) Father Lord, deliver me from this present trial, in the Name of Jesus.

2) Almighty Father, break me out of this present obscurity, in the Name of Jesus.

3) Holy Spirit, help me to overcome this trial, in Jesus Name.

4) Holy Spirit, speak to me, in the Name of Jesus.

5) Holy Spirit, minister to my subconscious spirit, in the Name of Jesus.

6) Fire of God, burn down every mountain of difficulty, in the Name of Jesus.

7) Holy Ghost, baptize me with your fire, in the Name of Jesus.

8) Holy Spirit, go before me and favor me in this present challenge, in the Name of Jesus.

9) Spirit of God, grant me liberty and freedom by the fire of the Holy Spirit, in the Name of Jesus.

10) Father Lord, intervene on my behalf, in the Name of Jesus.

11) Ancient of day, liberate me this season, in the Name of Jesus.

12) Immortal redeemer, bring me higher above these prevailing changes.

13) Lord God, turn this present obstacale into my miracle, in the Name of Jesus.

14) Fire of God, break down these obstacles for me, in the Name of Jesus.

15) Holy Spirit, favor me in, Jesus Name.

16) Holy Spirit. release me from this challenge, in the Name of Jesus.

17) Holy Spirit, become my compionion, in Jesus Name.

18) Holy Spirit, represent me in this matter.

19) Holy Spirit, elevant me beyond my own immagination, in the Name of Jesus.

20) Holy Spirit, do not allow my enemies to truimph over my life, in the Name of Jesus.

21) Fire of God, protect me, in the Name of Jesus.

22) Fire of God, destroy my enemies, in the Name of Jesus.

23) Fire of God, build a wall around me, in the Name of Jesus.

24) Fire of God, expose my enemies, in the Name of Jesus.

25) Fire of God, prove yourself, in the Name of Jesus.

26) Holy Spirit, represent me in jesus name.

27) Holy Spirit, release your boldnes into my life.

28) Holy Spirit, grant me signs and wonders.

29) Holy Spirit, make me a living wonder in my lifetime.

30) Holy Spirit, turn my life around, in the Name of Jesus.

31) Holy Spirit, I will not remain at this level, in the Name of Jesus.

32) Spirit of God, lift me higher, in the mighty Name of Jesus.

33) Angels of God, minister unto me, in the Name of Jesus.

34) Hand of God, separate me this season, in the Name of Jesus.

CONCLUSION

*And Caleb stilled the people before Moses,
and said, Let us go up at once, and possess it;
for we are well able to overcome it.*
Numbers 13:30

The mentality of fearless faith is a dominating force that has zero tolerance for intimidation and inferiority. We are assured of the backing and defense of the Almighty God. We must develop "the overcomer mentality" if we are to operate under the spirit of fearless faith. We must develop an "all possibility mentality"—despite the prevailing challenges, hardships or satanic assaults. *"Have not I commanded thee? Be strong and of a good courage; be not afraid, neither be thou dismayed: for the Lord thy God is with thee whithersoever thou goest."* (Joshua 1:9)

*Let us hear the conclusion of the whole matter:
Fear God, and keep his commandments: for this is the whole duty of man. For God shall bring every work into judgment, with every secret thing, whether it be good, or whether it be evil.*
Ecclesiastes 12:13-14

In my opinion, nothing changes around you unless there is a change of heart. All we have said will remain a story unless there is a conviction within your heart to obey God's commandments. The mysteries of God are provoked only when you fear God, Obey God, repent of all your unrighteous evil ways and seek the Lord forever more.

We must keep HIS commandments, for His commandments are not grievous, according to the Bible. *"For God shall bring every work into judgment, with every secret thing, whether it be good, or whether it be evil."* (Ecclesiastes 12:14) If you are a born again Christian we'd like to encourage you in your Christian life. If you are not a born again Christian, we can help you receive genuine salvation here.

Therefore if any man be in Christ, he is a new creature:
old things are passed away; behold,
all things are become new.
2 Corinthians 5:17

Now repeat this prayer after me:

Say Lord Jesus, I accept you today, as my Lord and my savior. Forgive me of my sins, wash me with your blood. Right now, I believe I am sanctified, I am saved, I am free. I am free from the power of sin, to serve the Lord Jesus. Thank you Lord for saving me. Amen.

Congratulations. You are now...

...a BORN AGAIN CHRISTIAN.

Again I say to you—CONGRATULATIONS!

What must I do to determine my divine visitation?

To determine divine visitation you must be born again! The word says as many as received him, to them gave He power to become the sons of God. Even to them that believe on his name.

To qualify for divine visitation, do the following sincerely:

1) Acknowledge that you are a sinner and that He died for you. (Romans 3:23)

2) Repent of your sins. (Acts 3:19, Luke 13:5, 2 Peter 3:9)

3) Believe in your heart that Jesus died for your sin. (Romans 10:10)

4) Confess Jesus as the Lord over your life. (Romans 10:10, Acts 2:21)

NOW REPEAT THIS PRAYER AFTER ME:

Say Lord Jesus, I accept you today, as my Lord and my savior, forgive me of my sins wash me with your blood. Right now, I believe, I am sanctified, I am save, I am free, I am free from the Power of sin to serve the Lord Jesus. Thank you Lord for saving me. Amen.

Congratulations. You are now...

...a BORN AGAIN CHRISTIAN.

Again I say to you—CONGRATULATIONS!

I adjure you to watch the Spirit of God bear witness with your Spirit confirming His word with signs following. The word says The Spirit itself beareth witness with our spirit, that we are the children of God. Join a Bible-believing church or join us on our weekly and Sunday worship services at 343 Sanford Avenue Newark, New Jersey 07106.

WISDOM KEYS

— Every productive society is a society heading to the top.

—Millions of Nigerians run away from Nigeria. Very few Nigerians stay in Nigeria.

—My decision to return Nigeria is the will of God for my life.

—My shortcoming in America after 18 years is the fact that I've trained me to be wise, to think, reflect and reason appropriately.

—If you train your mind to reason, it will train your hands to earn money.

—It is absurd to use the money of the heathen to build the kingdom of the living God.

—Every ministry reveals its agenda and VISION either at the beginning or at the end.

—Be careful of your life. It is your first ministry.

—The average American mind is conditioned for a continual quest to get new things and discard the old.

—When I considered well, my BMW jeep became my initial deposit for the work of the ministry in Nigeria.

—Money will never fall from any tree or person. Make up your mind to be independent today.

—Everyone is waiting for you to change your mind. Until you change your thinking, nothing changes around you.

—Multiple academic degrees in other disciplines gave me the chance to think and reason.

—Whatever anyone is thinking at any time reveals what is inside of their heart.

—All planned events are the product of meditation.

—Every event is designed for a designated timeline.

—Wisdom is your ability to think, to create and invent.

— If you can think wisely enough, you will come out of debt.

—The distance between you and your success is your innovative and creative ability to think well.

—Success is the result of hard work, commitment, resolve and determined learning from past mistakes and failings.

—If you organize your mind, you have organized your life and destiny.

—There is a thin line between success and failure.

—Wealth is your ability to think, power is your ability to reason and success is your ability to be informed.

—If you can make use of your mind by thinking and reasoning, God will make use of your life and destiny.

—Reflect, reason, think and be Great.

—Famous people are born of woman.

—That you will make it is your intention, that you will survive is your resolve, that you will succeed with changes is your determination, personal efforts and hard work.

—No man was born a failure.

—Lack of vision is the result of failure.

—Working with mental patients encourages and aspire me to be a productive observant and dedicated to my assignment.

—Successful people are not magicians. It is the will-power, combined with hard work and determination and a resolve to succeed, that make them succeed.

—In the unequivocal state of the mind, intention is not

a location or a position. It is the state of the mind.
—So many people think that they think.

—The mind is used to think, to reflect and to reason.

—You will remain blind with your eyes open until you can see with your mind by thinking.

—There is no favoritism in accurate and precise calculation.

—Although knowledge is power, information is the key and gateway to a great future.

—It will take the hand of God to move the hand of man.

—With the backing of the great wise God, nothing will disconnect you from your inheritance.

—As long as you have wisdom and understanding of God, Satan and evil cannot manipulate your life and destiny.

—You have come this far in life by your own judgment and the decisions you made in the past. Now lean in and listen to God for another dimension of greatness.

—Great people are ordinary people. It is extra ordinary efforts and the price of sacrifice that produces greatness in them.

—As a mental direct care worker, I saw a great pastor and a motivational speaker within myself.

—A menial job does not reduce your self-worth. Until you resolve to achieve greatness and see greatness in all you do, you will never count in your community.

—The principle of Jesus will solve your gambling and addiction problems.

—The man of Jesus will lead you into heaven.

—Everyone has their self-appraisal and what they think about you. Until you discover yourself, other opinions about you will alter the real you.

—Supervisors and directors are just a position in the chain of command in a workplace. Never allow your supervisor hierarchy to alter your opinion of yourself.

—Everyone can come out of debt if they make up their mind.

—The fact that I am not a decision-maker at work does not diminish my contribution to my world.

—Although it appears like it was a poor decision to accept a direct care employment at a psychiatric hospital, as I reflect on my nine years of that experience, it became apparent that I have learned and experienced enough for my next assignment.

—Self-encouragement and determination is a resolve of the heart.

—If you are determined to make a difference and do the things that make a difference, you will eventually make a difference.

—Good things do not come easy.

—Short cuts will cut your life short.

—Those who look ahead move ahead.

—Life is all about making an impact. In your lifetime strive to make an impact in your community.

—Make friends and connect with people who are moving ahead of you in life.

—If you can look around well, you have come a long way in your life, made a lot of difference and realized a lot of success in life.
—If you are my old friend, hurry up to reach out to me before I become a stranger to you.

—I am blessed with inspirations from God that changed

my interpretation of the world around me.

—I thought I was stagnant and lonely until I looked around and noticed my children running around and my wife cooking.

— At 40, I resigned my job to seek the Lord forever.

—My ministry took a drastic rise to the top when the wisdom of God visited me with knowledge and understanding.

—You will be a better person if you understand the characteristics of your personality like your mood swings, attitudes and habits.

—It is the seed of love you sow into the heart of a child and a woman that you reap in due time.

—Love is not selfish. Love shares everything, including the concealed secrets of the mind.

—As long as you have a prayer life and a Bible, you will never feel lonely in the race of life.

—When good friends disconnect from you, let them go. They might have seen something new in a different direction.

—Confidence in yourself and in God is the only way to

bring you out of captivity

—Never train a child to waste his or her time.

—The mind is the greatest asset of a great future.

—You walk by common sense, run by principles and fly by instruction.

—Those who become successful in life did it by self-determination, hard work and learning from past failures.

—Most successful people are lonely people. No one renders help to them, believing they are already successful. Except when they seek for more knowledge and information, they are all alone.

— I have seen a towing truck vehicle. I have also seen a towing ship in the water. But I have never seen a towing airplane in the air.

—I exercise my judgment and make a decision every minute of the day. Decisions are crucial, critical and vital with reference to your future.

—So many people wish for a great future. You can only work towards a great future.

—Your celebrity status began when you discovered your talent. What are you good at? Work at it with all your commitment.

—Prayers will sustain you, but the wisdom of God will prosper you.

—When I met Oyedepo, his teachings changed my perspective. But when I met Ibiyeomie, his teachings changed my perception.

— I will be successful in ministry if only I concentrate and focus my energy in the work of the ministry.

— It took the late Dr. Norman Vincent Peale's book to open my mind towards the kingdom of success.

CHAPTER 4
PRAYER OF SALVATION

I am glad you have read this book all the way from the beginning to this point. All I have said from the beginning will remain a mystery until you commit it into practice.

And before you do so, I want you—if you have not given your life to Jesus already—to do so now. Give your life to Christ. I want you to know the truth! The truth is that Jesus died for your sins and because He died, you must be alive and prosperous.

What must I do to determine my divine visitation?

To determine divine visitation, you must be born again! The word says, *"As many as received Him, to them gave He power to become the sons of God. Even to them that believe on his name."* (John 1:12)

To qualify for divine visitation, do the following with sincerity—

> 1) Acknowledge that you are a sinner and that He died for you. (Romans 3:23)
> 2) Repent of your sins. (Acts 3:19, Luke 13:5, 2 Peter 3:9)
> 3) Believe in your heart that Jesus died for your

sins. (Romans 10:10)
4) Confess Jesus as the Lord over your life. (Romans 10:10, Acts 2:21)

Now repeat this prayer after me:

Say Lord Jesus, I accept you today, as my Lord and my savior. Forgive me of my sins, wash me with your blood. Right now, I believe I am sanctified, I am saved, I am free. I am free from the power of sin, to serve the Lord Jesus. Thank you Lord for saving me. Amen.

Congratulations. You are now...

A BORN AGAIN CHRISTIAN.

Again I say to you—CONGRATULATIONS!

I adjure you to watch the Spirit of God bear witness with your Spirit, confirming His word with subsequent signs. The word says, *"The Spirit itself beareth witness with our spirit, that we are the children of God."* (Romans 8:16)

Chapter 4   Prayer of Salvation

MIRACLE CARE OUTREACH

*"...But that the members should have
the same care one for another"*
1 Corinthians 12:25

We are all members of the body of Christ. Jesus commanded us to love our neighbor as ourselves. This includes caring for one another as a member of one body. True love is expressed in caring and giving. The word says, for God so Love He gave….

Reach out to someone in need of Jesus. Help someone in crisis find Christ. Look out and prove your love to Jesus by caring and inviting your friends and associates to find Jesus the Healer.

Invite your friends to our Home Care Cell Fellowship (Miracle Chapel Intl. Satellite Fellowship). We're in the U.S. at 33 Schley Street, Newark, New Jersey 07112. Home Care Cell Fellowship Group meets every Tuesday at 6:00pm-7:00pm.

If you are in Nigeria—MIRACLE OF GOD MINISTRIES, aka "MIRACLE CHAPEL INTL." Mpama–Egbu-Owerri Imo state Nigeria.

LIFE IS NOT ALL ABOUT DURATION, BUT IT'S ALL ABOUT DONATION

What does this statement mean?
Life consists not in accumulation of material

wealth. (Luke 12:15) But it's all about liberality...i.e., what you can give and share with others. (Proverbs 11:25) When you live for others, you live forever—because you outlive your generation by the legacy you leave behind after you depart into glory to be with the Lord. But when you live for yourself, when you are reduced to SELF—you are easily forgotten when you die and depart in glory.

Permit me to admonish you today to live your life to be a blessing to a soul connected to you today. I want you to know that so many souls are connected and looking up to you, and through you so many souls will be saved and rescued from destruction. Will you disciple someone today to find Jesus Christ?

As a genuine Christian, it is your duty to evangelize Jesus Christ to all you meet on your way. Jesus is still in the healing business—Jesus is still doing miracles, from time of old to now. Therefore, tell someone about Jesus Christ today, disciple and bring them to Church. *Philip findeth Nathanael...* (John 1:45)

Please prove the sincerity of your love for God today, please become a soul winner. The dignity of your Christianity is hidden in your boldness to proclaim and evangelize Jesus Christ to all you meet on your way. There is a question mark on the integrity of your Christianity until you become a life soul winner. Invite someone to join us worship the Lord Jesus this coming Sunday. Amen.

MIRACLE OF GOD MINISTRIES
PILLARS OF THE COMMISSION

We Believe, Preach and Practice the following:

1) We believe and preach Salvation to every living human being.

2) We believe and preach Repentance and Forgiveness of sins.

3) We believe and preach the baptism of the Holy Spirit and Spiritual gifts.

4) We believe and teach Prosperity.

5) We believe and preach Divine Healing and Miracles—Signs and Wonder.

6) We believe and preach Faith.

7) We believe and proclaim the Power of God (Supernatural).

8) We believe and proclaim Praise and Worship to God.

9) We believe and preach Wisdom.

10) We believe and preach Holiness (Consecration).

11) We believe and preach Vision.

12) We believe and teach the Word of God.

13) We believe and teach Success.

14) We believe and practice Prayer.

15) We believe and teach Deliverance.

These 15 stones form the Pillars of Our Commission. Become part of this church family and follow this great move of God.

MY HEARTFELT PRAYER FOR YOU

It is my heart's desire for God to meet you through one of our teaching books and materials. It's also my personal desire for you to encounter God and receive the gift of Salvation.

Now let me Pray for you:

Spirit of the Living God, I come to you today with respect, reverence and humility. With a broken heart and a contrite Spirit I ask as an intercessor that you touch this precious loved one to whom you have given the privilege to read this book today. May their lives never remain the same. May your hand be established in their lives. Lord, bring comfort and assurance by your Holy Spirit. May they receive a divine infusion that will provoke the fearless spirit and the anointing of the Lord to fall upon them mightily. All these I pray, in the mighty name of Jesus. Amen.

FAVOR CONFESSION

Heavenly Father, I thank you for making me righteous and accepted through the blood of Jesus Christ. Because of that, I am blessed and highly favored by you. I am the object of your affection, fearfully and wonderfully made in your image. Your favor surrounds me as a shield. The first thing the people who come into contact with me see is your favor shield upon my life.

Thank you, Lord, today that I have favor with God and with man. Every day henceforth people go out of their way to bless me and favor me. I have favor with everyone that I deal with every day of my life. Opportunities that were once shut down are now open to me. I receive preferential treatment and I have special privileges—I am God's favored child. "No good thing will he withhold" from me as a result of God's favor upon my life. (Psalms 84:11) My enemies cannot triumph over me. I have supernatural increase and promotion. I declare restoration to everything that the devil has ever stolen from me in my lifetime. I have honor in the midst of my adversaries and an increase of asserts, especially in real estate and expansion of territories.

I am supernaturally favored by God in a wonderful way. I experience great victories, supernatural turnarounds and miraculous breakthroughs in the midst of great impossibilities. I receive recognition, prominence and honor. Petitions are granted to me, even by ungodly authorities. Policies, rules, protocols, regulations and laws are reversed and amended on my behalf. I win spiritual and physical battles that I don't even have to fight—my God fights them all for me. This is the day, the set time and the designated moment for me to experience the supernatural free favor of God that profusely and lavishly pours into my life. Amen.

ABOUT THE AUTHOR

Rev. Franklin N. Abazie is the founding and Presiding Pastor of Miracle of God Ministries, with headquarters in Newark, New Jersey USA and a branch church in Owerri-Imo State Nigeria. He is following the footsteps of one of his mentors, the healing evangelist Oral Roberts of the blessed memory. The Lord passed Oral Roberts' healing mantle two days before he went to be with the Lord at age 91 into the hands of healing evangelist Rev. Franklin N. Abazie in a vision.

In all his services, the Power and Presence of God is present to heal all in his audience. Rev. Abazie is an ordained man of God, with a Healing Ministry reviving the healing and miracle ministry of Jesus Christ of Nazareth.

Pastor Franklin N. Abazie, has been called by God with a unique mandate: **"THE MOMENT IS DUE TO IMPACT YOUR WORLD THROUGH THE REVIVAL OF THE HEALING AND MIRACLE MINISTRY OF JESUS CHRIST OF NAZARETH.**

"I AM SENDING YOU TO RESTORE HEALTH UNTO THEE AND I WILL HEAL THEE OF THY WOUNDS, SAID THE LORD OF HOST."

Rev. Abazie is a gifted, ardent teacher of the word of God, who operates also in the office of a Prophet, generating and attracting undeniable signs and wonders, special miracles and healings, with apostolic fireworks of the Holy Ghost. He is the founding and presiding senior Pastor of this fast growing Healing Ministry. He has written over 86 inspirational, healing and transforming books covering almost all aspects of divine healing and life. He is happily married and blessed with children.

BOOKS BY REV. FRANKLIN N. ABAZIE:

1) The Outcome of Faith
2) Understanding the Secret of Prevailing Prayers
3) Commanding Abundance
4) Understanding the Secret of the Man God Uses
5) Activating My Due Season
6) Overcoming Divine Verdicts
7) The Outcome of Divine Wisdom
8) Understanding God's Restoration Mandate
9) Walking In the Victory and Authority of the Truth
10) God's Covenant Exemption
11) Destiny Restoration Pillars
12) Provoking Acceptable Praise
13) Understanding Divine Judgment
14) Activating Angelic Re-enforcement
15) Provoking Un-Merited Favo
16) The Benefits of the Speaking Faith
17) Understanding Divine Arrangement
18) How to Keep Your Healing
19) Understanding the Mysteries of the Speaking Faith
20) Understanding the Mysteries of Prophetic Healing
21) Operating Under the Rules of Creative Healing
22) Understanding the Joy of Breakthrough
23) Understanding the Mystery of Breakthrough
24) Understanding Divine Prosperity
25) Understanding Divine Healing
26) Retaining Your Inheritance
27) Overcoming Confusing Spirit
28) Commanding Angelic Escorts

29) Enforcing Your Inheritance In Christ Jesus
30) Understanding Your Guardian Angels
31) Overcoming the Dominion of Sin
32) Understanding the Voice of God
33) The Outstanding Benefits of the Anointing
34) The Audacity of the Blood of Jesus
35) Walking in the Reality of the Anointing
36) Escaping the Nightmare of Poverty
37) Understanding Your Harvest Season
38) Activating Your Success Buttons
39) Overcoming the Forces of Darkness
40) Overcoming the Devices of the Devil
41) Overcoming Demonic Agents
42) Overcoming the Sorrows of Failure
43) Rejecting the Sorrows of Failure
44) Resisting the Sorrows of Poverty
45) Restoring Broken Marriages
46) Redeeming Your Days
47) The Force of Vision
48) Overcoming the Forces of Ignorance
49) Understanding the Sacrifice of Small Beginning
50) The Might of Small Beginning
51) Understanding the Mysteries of Prophesy
52) Overcoming Dream Nightmares
53) Breaking the Shackles of the Curse of the Law
54) Understanding the Joy of Harvest
55) Wisdom for Signs & Wonders
56) Wisdom for Generational Impact
57) Wisdom for Marriage Stability
58) Understanding the Number of Your Days

59) Enforcing Your Kingdom Rights
60) Escaping the Traps of Immoralities
61) Escaping the Trap of Poverty
62) Accessing Biblical Prosperity
63) Accessing True Riches in Christ
64) Silencing the Voice of the Accuser
65) Overcoming the Forces of Oppositions
66) Quenching the Voice of the Avenger
67) Silencing Demonic Prediction & Projection
68) Silencing Your Mocker
69) Understanding the Power of the Holy Ghost
70) Understanding the Baptism of Power
71) The Mystery of the Blood of Jesus
72) Understanding the Mystery of Sanctification
73) Understanding the Power of Holiness
74) Understanding the Forces of Purity & Righteousness
75) Activating the Forces of Vengeance
76) Appreciating the Mystery of Restoration
77) Overcoming the Projection & Prediction of the Enemy
78) Engaging the Mystery of the Blood
79) Commanding the Power of the Speaking Faith
80) Uprooting the Forces Against Your Rising
81) Overcoming Mere Success Syndrome
82) Understanding Divine Sentence
83) Understanding the Mystery of Praise
84) Understanding the Author of Faith
85) The Mystery of the Finisher of Faith
86) Attracting Supernatural Favor

MIRACLE OF GOD MINISTRIES
NIGERIA CRUSADE 2012

MIRACLE OF GOD MINISTRIES
NIGERIA CRUSADE
2012

MIRACLE OF GOD MINISTRIES
NIGERIA CRUSADE 2012

MIRACLE OF GOD MINISTRIES

NIGERIA CRUSADE

2012

MIRACLE OF GOD MINISTRIES

NIGERIA CRUSADE

2012

www.ingramcontent.com/pod-product-compliance
Lightning Source LLC
Chambersburg PA
CBHW021446080526
44588CB00009B/713